# SANSKRIT WORKBOOK
## Learning the Alphabet

Thomas Egenes, Ph.D.

To be used with the text **Introduction to Sanskrit** by Thomas Egenes

# MAHARISHI INTERNATIONAL
# UNIVERSITY PRESS

ISBN 0-923569-09-X

Maharishi International University Press, Fairfield, Iowa, U.S.A.

# TABLE OF CONTENTS

**HOW TO USE
THIS WORKBOOK**

This workbook should be used with the textbook **Introduction to Sanskrit**. The lessons in the workbook correspond primarily to the following lessons on the **devanāgarī** script in **Introduction to Sanskrit**:

| Sanskrit Workbook | Introduction to Sanskrit |
|---|---|
| **Lesson One** | **Lesson One**, pp. 2-4 |
| **Lesson Two** | **Lesson Two**, p. 12 (also Lesson One, pp. 2-4) |
| **Lesson Three** | **Lesson Three**, p. 23 (also Lesson Two, pp. 9 & 10) |
| **Lesson Four** | **Lesson Four**, p. 32 (also Lesson Two, pp. 9-11) |
| **Lesson Five** | **Lesson Five**, p. 42-44 (also Lesson Two, pp. 9-11) (also Lesson Three, pp. 19-22) |
| **Lesson Six** | **Lesson Six**, pp. 55-57 |
| **Lesson Seven** | **Lesson Seven**, pp. 68-71 |

**GUIDELINES
FOR STUDYING**

Here are some guidelines for learning the alphabet. The key to learning the alphabet is repetition. Review as often as possible during the day, taking a few minutes to bring the material to mind If there is any hesitation in recall, immediately look at the answers on the back of each page.  Review often and out loud, if possible. Memorization should be easy, comfortable, and frequent.

**PRONUNCIATION**

The Sanskrit alphabet can be formed with 52 letters, as described in this workbook. (The alphabet can be formed in more than one way, because a few letters are not used very often.)  Pronounce the letters in a relaxed and natural way, without straining.  Use the audio tape available with this workbook, as imitating the pronunciation of a qualified person is helpful.  The section of the Vedic literature that teaches correct pronunciation of the alphabet is **Śikṣā**, the first of the six **Vedāṅgas**.  One of the texts of **Śikṣā** states that Sanskrit should be pronounced with sweetness, clearness, and patience (**Pāṇinīya Śikṣā**, 33).

**ACKNOWLEDGEMENTS**

Inspiration, suggestions, and assistance have come from the following individuals:  Michael Davis, Carol DeGiere, Shepley Hansen, and Craig Pearson.  My wife, Linda, assisted in editing and offered continuous guidance and support. The section of this workbook entitled "Reading from the **Bhagavad-Gītā**" includes selections from Maharishi's translation of the **Bhagavad-Gītā**.

**DEDICATION**

This workbook is dedicated with appreciation and gratitude to His Holiness Maharishi Mahesh Yogi, who has described Sanskrit as the language of nature, the language of the impulses of the unified field of natural law. Maharishi has explained how the ancient rishis of the Himalayas cognized, in their silent meditations, impulses within pure consciousness. These cognitions were recorded in the Vedic literature, a vast body of beautiful and exhilarating expressions that describe the mechanics of evolution in every field of life.

Maharishi has emphasized the value of learning the 52 letters of the Sanskrit alphabet and learning to read the Vedic literature in the original script. Calling it a "formula for perfection," Maharishi has stated that pronouncing the sounds of the Vedic literature produces a corresponding quality in consciousness and through consciousness in the physiology and environment.

Maharishi has taught, from the Vedic tradition, practical procedures for unfolding evolution in daily life. These techniques have brought happiness and satisfaction to millions of people around the world and have been verified by hundreds of scientific studies on every continent. Maharishi has not only provided the means for removing stress and suffering, but for unfolding the full potential within every individual and creating perfect health, progress, prosperity, and permanent peace for the world.

# LESSON

# ONE

## THE VOWELS

Refer to **Introduction to Sanskrit** text, pp. 2-4.

Pronounce this letter (the answer is on the back of this page):

Now write the letter many times, pronouncing it as you write:

**a** like the first "a" in <u>A</u>merica

Pronounce this letter:

Now write the letter many times, pronouncing it as you write:

ā like the "a" in fa̱ther

Pronounce this letter:

Now write the letter many times, pronouncing it as you write:

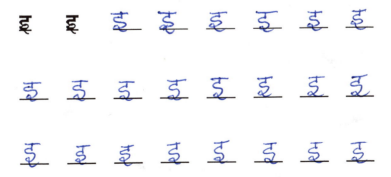

i like the "i" in the word "i̲n̲"

Pronounce this letter:

Now write the letter many times:

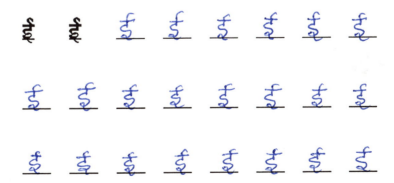

ī  like the "ee" in b<u>ee</u>t

Pronounce this letter:

Now write the letter many times:

ॐ  ॐ  __  ___  ___  ___  ___  ___  ___

___  ___  ___  ___  ___  ___  ___  ___

___  ___  ___  ___  ___  ___  ___  ___

**u** like the "u" in s<u>ui</u>t

Pronounce this letter:

Now write the letter many times:

ॐ    ॐ    __ __ __ __ __ __ __

__ __ __ __ __ __ __ __

__ __ __ __ __ __ __ __

ū  like the "oo" in p<u>oo</u>l

**REVIEW**
Now practice pronouncing all the letters you have learned.  Go across and then up and down until you can read them in any order easily:

अ       ऊ       इ

उ       आ       ई

इ       ऊ       अ

Answers:

a            ū            i

u            ā            ī

i            ū            a

# LESSON TWO
**MORE VOWELS**

Refer to **Introduction to Sanskrit**, p. 12 (also pp. 2-4).

Pronounce this letter:

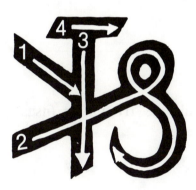

Now write the letter many times:

ऋ ऋ __ __ __ __ __ __

__ __ __ __ __ __ __

__ __ __ __ __ __ __

ṛ  like the "ri" in  river  (usually not rolled)

Pronounce this letter:

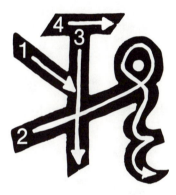

Now write the letter many times:

丞 丞 __ __ __ __ __ __

__ __ __ __ __ __ __

__ __ __ __ __ __ __

ṝ  like the "ri" in <u>ri</u>ver (held longer than ṛ)

Pronounce this letter:

Now write the letter many times:

ऌ   ऌ   —  —  —  —  —  —  —

—  —  —  —  —  —  —

—  —  —  —  —  —  —

ı like the "lry" in jewel<u>ry</u>

Pronounce this letter:

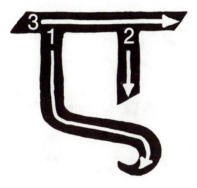

Now write the letter many times:

ए    ए    —   —   —   —   —   —

—   —   —   —   —   —   —

—   —   —   —   —   —   —

**e**  like the "a" in  g<u>a</u>te

Pronounce this letter:

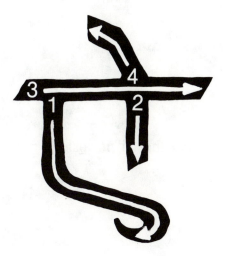

Now write the letter many times:

ऐ    ऐ    —    —    —    —    —    —

—    —    —    —    —    —    —

—    —    —    —    —    —    —

**ai**  like the "ai" in <u>ai</u>sle

Pronounce this letter:

Now write the letter many times:

ओ  ओ  __  __  __  __  __  __

__  __  __  __  __  __

__  __  __  __  __  __

o like the "o" in p<u>o</u>le

Pronounce this letter:

Now write the letter many times:

औ  औ  __ __ __ __ __ __ __

__ __ __ __ __ __ __ __

__ __ __ __ __ __ __ __

**au** like the "ou" in l<u>ou</u>d

**REVIEW**          Now let's practice pronouncing the letters you have learned.  Test
                    yourself by reading across and then up and down until you can read
                    them in any order easily:

| | | | |
|:---:|:---:|:---:|:---:|
| अ | ऋ | ए | औ |
| आ | उ | ओ | ल |
| इ | ऊ | ई | ऋ |
| ऋ | ऐ | औ | ऊ |

Answers:

| a | ṛ | e | au |
|---|---|---|----|
| ā | u | o | ḷ |
| i | ū | ī | ṝ |
| ṛ | ai | au | ū |

# LESSON
# THREE
**THE CONSONANTS**

Refer to **Introduction to Sanskrit**, p. 23 (also pp. 9 & 10).

Pronounce this letter:

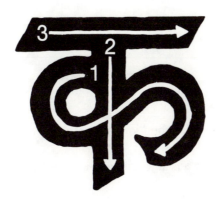

Now write the letter many times:

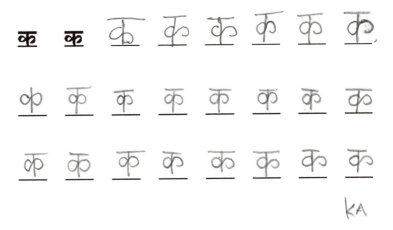

KA

ka

**k**  like the "k" in s<u>k</u>ate

The **a** is automatically included with each consonant.  क = **ka**

Pronounce this letter:

Now write the letter many times:

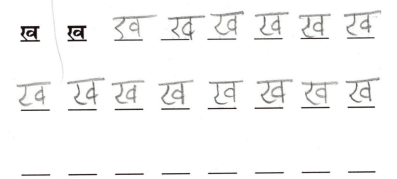

— — — — — — — —

kha

**kh**  like the "kh" in bun<u>kh</u>ouse

Pronounce this letter:

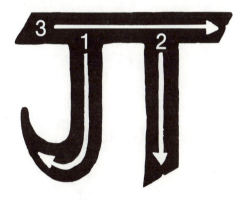

Now write the letter many times:

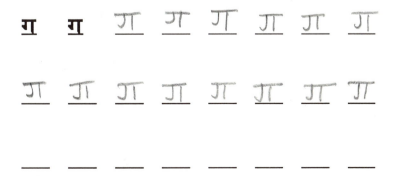

$g$a

$g$  like the "g" in  go

Pronounce this letter:

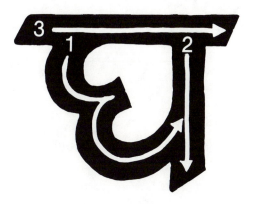

Now write the letter many times:

घ  घ  घ घ घ घ घ घ घ

घ घ घ घ घ घ घ घ

— — — — — — — —

gha

**gh** like the "gh" in lo<u>gh</u>ouse

Pronounce this letter:

Now write the letter many times:

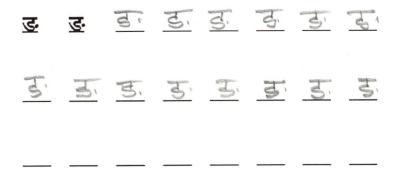

ña

ñ  like the "n" in si<u>ng</u>

Pronounce this letter:

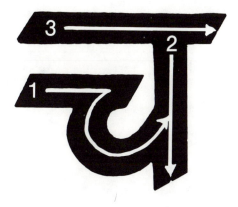

Now write the letter many times:

च  च  ___  ___  ___  ___  ___  ___

___  ___  ___  ___  ___  ___  ___

___  ___  ___  ___  ___  ___  ___

**ca**

**c**  like the "c" in c̲ello

Pronounce this letter:

Now write the letter many times:

ত   ত   ___  ___  ___  ___  ___  ___

___  ___  ___  ___  ___  ___  ___  ___

___  ___  ___  ___  ___  ___  ___  ___

**cha**

**ch** like the "ch" in <u>ch</u>arm (using more breath)

Pronounce this letter:

Now write the letter many times:

ज  ज  __ __ __ __ __ __

__ __ __ __ __ __

__ __ __ __ __ __

ja

j  like the "j" in  just

Pronounce this letter:

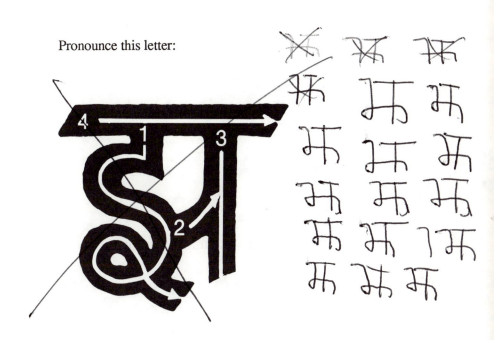

Now write the letter many times:

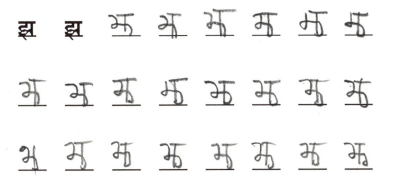

jha

**jh** like the "jh" in just (using more breath)

Pronounce this letter:

Now write the letter many times:

अ   अ   अ अ अ अ अ अ

अ अ अ अ अ अ अ अ अ

अ अ अ अ अ अ अ अ

ña

ñ  like the "n" in  enjoyable

**REVIEW**

Now test yourself by pronouncing the letters you have learned. Practice reading left to right and in other orders until you can easily read the entire chart:

क    ग    घ    ञ    इ    छ

अ    उ    ऋ    औ    ज    क

ए    ऐ    ओ    इ    क    ऋ

घ    ग    ञ    छ    उ    ऋ

आ    ओ    क    ज    च    ङ

च    ऐ    औ    ऊ    ज    झ

Answers:

| ka | ga | gha | ña | i | cha |
|---|---|---|---|---|---|
| a | u | ṛ | au | ja | ka |
| e | ai | o | i | ka | ṝ |
| gha | ga | ña | cha | u | ṛ |
| ā | o | ka | ja | ca | ña |
| ca | ai | au | ū | ja | jha |

# LESSON FOUR

**MORE CONSONANTS**

Refer to **Introduction to Sanskrit**, p. 32 (also pp. 9-11).

Pronounce this letter:

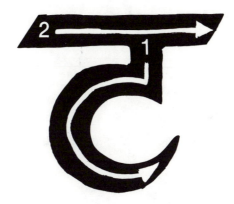

Now write the letter many times:

ट     ट     —   —   —   —   —   —

—   —   —   —   —   —   —

—   —   —   —   —   —   —

ṭa

ṭ  like the "t" in sṯable (tongue touching hard palate)

Pronounce this letter:

Now write the letter many times:

ō    ō    __  __  __  __  __  __

__  __  __  __  __  __  __

__  __  __  __  __  __  __

ṭha

ṭh  like the "t" in ṭable (using more breath, tongue
                                    touching hard palate)

Pronounce this letter:

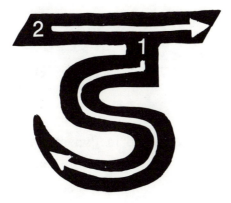

Now write the letter many times:

ड      ड      __  __  __  __  __  __

__  __  __  __  __  __

__  __  __  __  __  __

ḍa

ḍ like the "d" in <u>d</u>ynamic (tongue touching hard palate)

Pronounce this letter:

Now write the letter many times:

ळ   ळ   __ __ __ __ __ __

__ __ __ __ __ __ __

__ __ __ __ __ __

ḷa

ḷ  like the "l" in ḻake (tongue touching hard palate)

The retroflex ḷa is used sometimes in Vedic Sanskrit instead of ḍa.
The ḷa is used between two vowels.  For example:

## अग्निमीळे

agnim īḷe

This Vedic letter is not discussed in the text **Introduction to Sanskrit.**

Pronounce this letter:

Now write the letter many times:

ত   ত   ___  ___  ___  ___  ___  ___

___  ___  ___  ___  ___  ___  ___

___  ___  ___  ___  ___  ___  ___

ḍha

**ḍh** like the "dh" in re<u>dh</u>ead (tongue touching hard
palate)

Pronounce this letter:

Now write the letter many times:

ಞ  ಞ  __ __ __ __ __ __ __ __

__ __ __ __ __ __ __ __

__ __ __ __ __ __ __ __

ḷha

ḷh  like the "l" in ḷake (tongue touching hard palate,
                                using more breath)

The retroflex ḷha is used sometimes in Vedic Sanskrit instead of
ḍha. The ḷha is used between two vowels.

This Vedic letter is not discussed in the text **Introduction to
Sanskrit**.

Pronounce this letter:

Now write the letter many times:

ण    ण    —   —   —   —   —   —

—   —   —   —   —   —   —   —

—   —   —   —   —   —   —   —

ṇa

ṇ  like the "n" in  geṉtle (tongue touching hard palate)

Pronounce this letter:

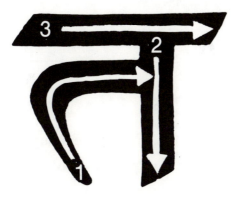

Now write the letter many times:

त  त  __ __ __ __ __ __

__ __ __ __ __ __ __

__ __ __ __ __ __ __

**ta**

**t** like the "t" in st̲able  (tongue at base of teeth)

Pronounce this letter:

Now write the letter many times:

थ   थ   __ __ __ __ __ __

__ __ __ __ __ __ __

__ __ __ __ __ __ __

**tha**

**th**  like the "t" in ṯable  (using more breath, tongue at
base of teeth)

Pronounce this letter:

Now write the letter many times:

द्  द्  —  —  —  —  —  —

—  —  —  —  —  —  —

—  —  —  —  —  —  —

da

**d** like the "d" in <u>d</u>ynamic (tongue at base of teeth)

Pronounce this letter:

Now write the letter many times:

ध ध _ _ _ _ _ _

_ _ _ _ _ _ _

_ _ _ _ _ _ _

dha

**dh** like the "dh" in re<u>dh</u>ead (tongue at base of teeth)

Pronounce this letter:

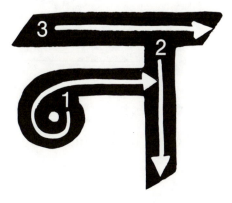

Now write the letter many times:

न  न  ___  ___  ___  ___  ___

___  ___  ___  ___  ___

___  ___  ___  ___  ___

na

**n** like the "n" in ge<u>n</u>tle (tongue at base of teeth)

**REVIEW**   Pronounce the following letters:

ढ    थ    ध    ठ    क    न    ण

च    अ    ज    ई    ऋ    ट    न

त    थ    ए    ओ    द्    ढ    औ

ध    घ    छ    झ    ऊ    ऋ    थ

द्    त    थ    ळ    ण    ट    ज

Answers:

| | | | | | | |
|---|---|---|---|---|---|---|
| ḍha | tha | dha | ṭha | ka | na | ṇa |
| ca | a | ja | ī | ṛ | ṭa | na |
| ta | tha | e | o | da | ḍha | au |
| dha | gha | cha | jha | ū | ṝ | tha |
| da | ta | tha | ḷ | ṇa | ṭa | ja |

# LESSON

# FIVE

**MORE CONSONANTS**
**SEMI-VOWELS**
**SIBILANTS**

Refer to **Introduction to Sanskrit**, pp. 42-44 (also pp. 9-11 & 19-22).

Pronounce this letter:

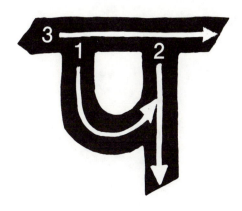

Now write the letter many times:

प    प    ___  ___  ___  ___  ___  ___

___  ___  ___  ___  ___  ___

___  ___  ___  ___  ___  ___

pa

**p** like the "p" in spin

Pronounce this letter:

Now write the letter many times:

फ  फ  __  __  __  __  __  __

__  __  __  __  __  __

__  __  __  __  __  __

pha

**ph** like the "ph" in she<u>ph</u>erd

Pronounce this letter:

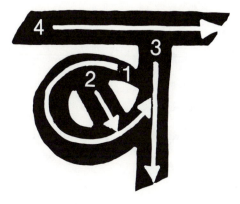

Now write the letter many times:

ब    ब    __  __  __  __  __  __  __

__  __  __  __  __  __  __  __

__  __  __  __  __  __  __  __

ba

ᑲ like the "b" in ᗷeautiful

Pronounce this letter:

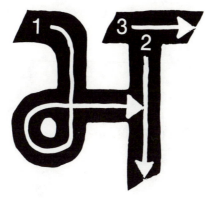

Now write the letter many times:

ਮ   ਮ   __  __  __  __  __  __

__  __  __  __  __  __

__  __  __  __  __  __

bha

**bh** like the "bh" in clu<u>bh</u>ouse

Pronounce this letter:

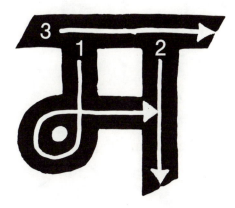

Now write the letter many times:

म   म   __  __  __  __  __  __

__  __  __  __  __  __  __

__  __  __  __  __  __  __

**ma**

**m** like the "m" in <u>m</u>other

Pronounce this letter:

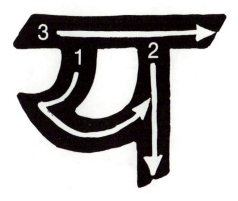

Now write the letter many times:

य   य ___ ___ ___ ___ ___ ___ ___

___ ___ ___ ___ ___ ___

___ ___ ___ ___ ___ ___

**ya**
**y** like the "y" in y̲es

Pronounce this letter:

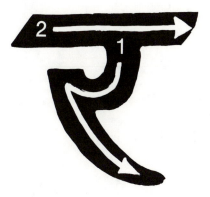

Now write the letter many times:

**ra**

**r** like the "r" in <u>r</u>ed

Pronounce this letter:

Now write the letter many times:

ড  ড  __  __  __  __  __  __

__  __  __  __  __  __  __

__  __  __  __  __  __  __

**la**

l   like the "l" in law

Pronounce this letter:

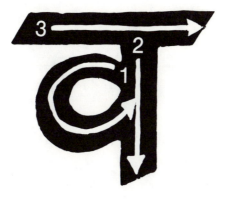

Now write the letter many times:

व   व   __ __ __ __ __ __

__ __ __ __ __ __ __

__ __ __ __ __ __ __

**va**

**v**  like the "v" in <u>v</u>ictory (but closer to a "w")

Pronounce this letter:

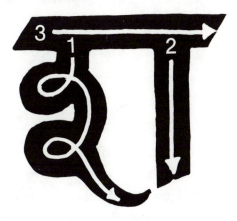

Now write the letter many times:

श  श  — — — — — — —

— — — — — — — —

— — — — — — — —

śa

**ś** like the "sh" in <u>sh</u>ine

This is pronounced at the same point of contact as **ca**. See **Introduction to Sanskrit**, p. 21, number 10.

Pronounce this letter:

Now write the letter many times:

ष  ष  __  __  __  __  __  __

__  __  __  __  __  __  __

__  __  __  __  __  __  __

ṣa

ṣ  like the "c" in effiçient

This is pronounced at the same point of contact as ṭa. See
**Introduction to Sanskrit**, p. 21, number 10.

Pronounce this letter:

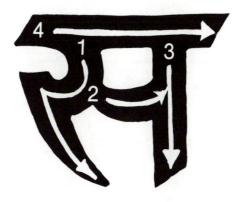

Now write the letter many times:

स   स  —  —  —  —  —  —  —

—  —  —  —  —  —  —  —

—  —  —  —  —  —  —

**sa**

**s** like the "s" in <u>s</u>weet

Pronounce this letter:

Now write the letter many times:

ह   ह   ——  ——  ——  ——  ——  ——

——  ——  ——  ——  ——  ——  ——

——  ——  ——  ——  ——  ——  ——

ha

**h** like the "h" in <u>h</u>ero

Pronounce these letters:

Now write the letters many times:

अं  अं __ __ __ __ __ __

अं  =  aṃ

The ṃ is called **anusvāra**.  It causes the last portion of the vowel before it to be nasal (like the French word "bon").  The **anusvāra** changes its sound according to its environment.  It sounds like the nasal of the set to which the sound following it belongs.  For example, **Saṃkara** is pronounced like **Śaṅkara** (with more nasalization of the first **a**), and **Saṃhitā** is pronounced like **Sañhitā** (with more nasalization of the **a**).

गं  =  gaṃ

तं  =  taṃ

सं  =  saṃ

Pronounce these letters:

Now write the letters many times:

अः अः __ __ __ __ __

__ __ __ __ __ __ __

__ __ __ __ __ __ __

अ:  = aḥ

The ḥ is called **visarga.** It is an unvoiced breathing, usually at the end of a word. For example, **yogasthaḥ** (established in yoga).

Pronounce these letters:

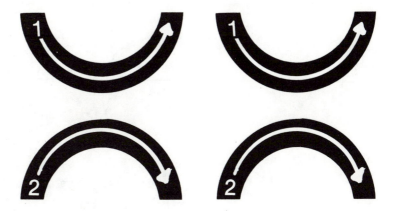

Now write the letters many times:

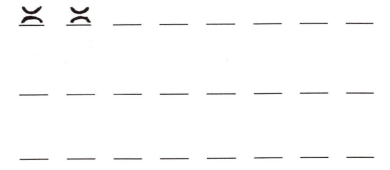

$$\asymp = \underline{h}$$

$$\asymp = \underset{\smile}{h}$$

The $\underline{h}$ is called **jihvāmūlīya**. It is sometimes used in place of a **visarga** before **ka** or **kha**.

The $\underset{\smile}{h}$ is called **upadhmānīya**. It is sometimes used in place of a **visarga** before **pa** or **pha**.

These Vedic letters are written the same way, but called **jihvāmūlīya** when placed before **ka** or **kha**, and **upadhmānīya** when placed before **pa** or **pha**.

**REVIEW**        Pronounce the following letters:

अ फ ब र स ल

ह क ष ड ढ न

श य प भ म थ

ज छ घ ए उ व

ग ख ह ल र म

फ प श ष स र

Answers:

| a | pha | ba | ra | sa | la |
|---|-----|----|----|-----|----|
| ha | ka | ṣa | ḍa | ḍha | na |
| śa | ya | pa | bha | ma | tha |
| ja | cha | gha | e | u | va |
| ga | kha | ha | la | ra | ma |
| pha | pa | śa | ṣa | sa | ra |

# LESSON

## SIX

**VOWELS AFTER CONSONANTS**

Pronounce these letters:

गा

Now write the letters many times:

गा गा __ __ __ __ __ __ __

__ __ __ __ __ __ __ __

__ __ __ __ __ __ __ __

गा   = g**ā** (like the "go" in g<u>o</u>t)

Pronounce these letters:

Now write the letters many times:

गि  गि  __  __  __  __  __  __

__  __  __  __  __  __  __  __

__  __  __  __  __  __  __  __

गि  = **g**i  (like the "gi" in g<u>i</u>ft)

When typed, the curved line on top may not touch the horizontal
bar.  For example:

गि

When written by hand, the curved line should touch the horizontal
bar at the point where it meets the vertical line.  For example:

गि

Pronounce these letters:

Now write the letters many times:

गी   गी __ __ __ __ __ __

— — — — — — —

— — — — — — —

गी  = gī (like the "gee" in ge_e_se)

Pronounce these letters:

Now write the letters many times:

गु  गु  — — — — — —

— — — — — — —

— — — — — — —

गु  = **gu** (like the "goo" in g<u>oo</u>se)

Pronounce these letters:

Now write the letters many times:

गू गू — — — — — — —

— — — — — — —

— — — — — — —

गू = *gū* (like the "goo" in <u>goo</u>se, only held longer)

Pronounce these letters:

Now write the letters many times:

गृ   गृ   —   —   —   —   —   —

—   —   —   —   —   —   —

—   —   —   —   —   —   —

ऋ = gṛ (like the "gri" in g<u>ri</u>p)

Pronounce these letters:

Now write the letters many times:

गृ  गृ  —  —  —  —  —  —  —

—  —  —  —  —  —  —

—  —  —  —  —  —  —

ॠ  =  **gr̄** (like the "gri" in <u>gri</u>p, only held longer)

Pronounce these letters:

Now write the letters many times:

गे   गे  __  __  __  __  __  __  __

___  __  __  __  __  __  __  __

__  __  __  __  __  __  __  __

गे  = **ge** like the "ga" in g<u>a</u>te

Pronounce these letters:

Now write the letters many times:

गै   गै __ __ __ __ __ __ __

__ __ __ __ __ __ __

__ __ __ __ __ __ __

गै = *gai* (like the word "guy")

Pronounce these letters:

Now write the letters many times:

गो  गो  __ __ __ __ __ __

__ __ __ __ __ __ __

__ __ __ __ __ __ __

गो  = **go**  (like the English word "go")

Pronounce these letters:

Now write the letters many times:

गौ  गौ __ __ __ __ __ __

__ __ __ __ __ __ __

__ __ __ __ __ __ __

गौ = **gau** (like the "gow" in <u>gow</u>n)

Pronounce these letters:

Now write the letters many times:

ক  ক  ___  ___  ___  ___  ___  ___

___  ___  ___  ___  ___  ___  ___

___  ___  ___  ___  ___  ___  ___

 रु  = **ru** (like the "roo" in <u>root</u>)

Pronounce these letters:

Now write the letters many times:

रू = rū (like the "ru" in r<u>u</u>le)

Pronounce these letters:

Now write the letters many times:

ह्रु   ह्रु   ___  ___  ___  ___  ___  ___  ___

___  ___  ___  ___  ___  ___  ___  ___

___  ___  ___  ___  ___  ___  ___  ___

ह्र = hṛ (like the "hri" in the Sanskrit word

hṛdayam, heart)

Pronounce these letters:

च्    चा    चि    ची

Now write the letters many times:

च् चा चि ची __ __ __ __

__ __ __ __ __ __ __ __

__ __ __ __ __ __ __ __

Answers:

च् = c

चा = cā

चि = ci

ची = cī

Pronounce these letters:

पे   पै   पो   पौ

Now write the letters many times:

<u>पे</u>   <u>पै</u>   <u>पो</u>   <u>पौ</u>  __   __   __   __

__   __   __   __   __   __   __

__   __   __   __   __   __   __

Answers:

पे = pe

पै = pai

पो = po

पौ = pau

Pronounce these letters:

अ हो गा नि रा म

सी ता खा औ तु जि

गी ता फ ल भू नृ

ऋ षि इ ति हा स

ए व ज य ते ह

Answers:

| a  | ho | gā  | ni  | rā  | ma |
|----|----|-----|-----|-----|----|
| sī | tā | khā | au  | tu  | ji |
| gī | tā | pha | la  | bhū | nṛ |
| ṛ  | ṣi | i   | ti  | hā  | sa |
| e  | va | ja  | ya  | te  | ha |

Pronounce this word:

राम

Now write the word many times:

राम  राम __ __ __ __ __ __

__ __ __ __ __ __ __

__ __ __ __ __ __ __

Answer:

राम  =  Rāma

Each syllable ends with a vowel.  For example:

रा म  =  Rā ma

Pronounce this word:

सीता

Now write the word many times:

सीता  __  __  __  __  __  __  __

__  __  __  __  __  __  __  __

__  __  __  __  __  __  __  __

Answer:

सीता  = Sītā

सी ता  = Sī tā

Pronounce these words:

# जय गुरु देव

Now write the words many times:

जय गुरु देव __ __ __ __ __ __

__ __ __ __ __ __ __

__ __ __ __ __ __ __

Answer:

जय गुरु देव  = Jaya Guru Deva

Pronounce this word:

महाभारत

Now write the word many times:

महाभारत _____    _____    _____

_____    _____    _____    _____

_____    _____    _____    _____

Answer:

महाभारत  = Mahābhārata

म हा भा र त  = Ma hā bhā ra ta

Pronounce this word:

संहिता

Now write the letters many times:

संहिता —————  —————  —————

—————  —————  —————  —————

—————  —————  —————  —————

Answer:

**संहिता** = Saṃhitā

Syllables can also end with **anusvāra** (ṃ) or **visarga** (ḥ).  For example:

**सं हि ता** = Saṃ hi tā

Pronounce these words:

पुराण

इतिहास

रामायण

उपनिषद्

वैशेषिक

योग

Answers:

**Purāṇa**

**Itihāsa**

**Rāmāyaṇa**

**Upaniṣad**

**Vaiśeṣika**

**Yoga**

# LESSON
# SEVEN
**CONJUNCT**
**CONSONANTS**

Refer to **Introduction to Sanskrit**, pp. 68-71.

Pronounce the following combinations of letters:

| | |
|---|---|
| त्य | स्थ |
| ण्य | ग्न |
| च्छ | प्त |
| ष्य | ल्प |
| ज्य | न्य |
| न्त | क्ल |

Answers:

| | |
|---|---|
| tya | stha |
| vya | gna |
| ccha | pta |
| ṣya | lpa |
| jya | nya |
| nta | kla |

Pronounce the following groups of letters and words:

| | |
|---|---|
| न्या | न्याय |
| ०्या | ०्याकरण |
| ज्यो | ज्योतिष |
| न्त | वेदान्त |
| ल्प | कल्प |
| ग्नि | अग्नि |
| स्था | स्थापत्य |

Answers:

| | |
|---|---|
| nyā | Nyāya   (Nyā ya) |
| vyā | Vyākaraṇa (Vyā ka ra ṇa) |
| jyo | Jyotiṣa   (Jyo ti ṣa) |
| nta | Vedānta  (Ve dā nta) |
| lpa | Kalpa  (Ka lpa) |
| gni | Agni  (A gni) |
| sthā | Sthāpatya  (Sthā pa tya) |

Pronounce the following letters and words:

| | |
|---|---|
| ङ्ञ | वेदाङ्ग |
| द्व | द्वन्द्व |
| द्धि | सिद्धि |
| ष्टा | अष्टाङ्ग |
| सो | सोम |
| सं | संयम |
| न्द् | आनन्द् |
| स्कृ | संस्कृत |
| क्त | अव्यक्त |
| द्री | भगवद्रीता |

Answers:

| | |
|---|---|
| ṅga | Vedāṅga |
| dva | dvandva |
| ddhi | siddhi |
| ṣṭā | aṣṭāṅga |
| so | soma |
| saṃ | saṃyama |
| nda | ānanda |
| skṛ | Saṃskṛta |
| kta | avyakta |
| dgī | Bhagavad-Gītā |

Pronounce the following letters and words:

| | |
|---|---|
| त्म | आत्मन् |
| ध्या | ध्यान |
| त्य | नित्य |
| न्द | छन्दस् |
| दुः | दुःख |
| स्य | रहस्य |
| ष्ण | कृष्ण |
| ली | लीला |
| रू | नामरूप |
| ङ्ञा | गङ्ञा |

Answers:

| | |
|---|---|
| tma | ātman |
| dhyā | dhyāna |
| tya | nitya |
| nda | chandas |
| duḥ | duḥkha |
| sya | rahasya |
| ṣṇa | Kṛṣṇa |
| lī | līlā |
| rū | nāma-rūpa |
| ṅgā | Gaṅgā |

Pronounce the following letters and words:

| | |
|---|---|
| र्म | कर्म |
| र्श | दर्शन |
| प्र | प्रकृति |
| र्य | सूर्य |
| स्का | नमस्कार |
| र्म | धर्म |
| ब्र | ब्रह्मन् |
| प्रा | प्राण |
| न्ति | शान्ति |
| तु | तुरीय |

Answers:

| | |
|---|---|
| rma | karma |
| rśa | darśana |
| pra | prakṛti |
| rya | sūrya |
| skā | namaskāra |
| rma | dharma |
| bra | brahman |
| prā | prāṇa |
| nti | śānti |
| tu | turīya |

Pronounce the following letters and words:

| | |
|---|---|
| त्र | सूत्र |
| क्ष | क्षत्रिय |
| त्त | चित्त |
| त्त्व | तत्त्व |
| द्या | विद्या |
| ज्ञा | प्रज्ञा |
| क्ति | भक्ति |
| द्र | चन्द्र |
| ध्या | ध्यान |
| र्य | आचार्य |

Answers:

| | |
|---|---|
| tra | sūtra |
| kṣa | kṣatriya |
| tta | citta |
| ttva | tattva |
| dyā | vidyā |
| jñā | prajñā |
| kti | bhakti |
| dra | candra |
| dhyā | dhyāna |
| rya | ācārya |

**REVIEW**                   Pronounce the following words:

1. ऋषि                          13. चित्तवृत्ति

2. आसन                        14. अविद्या

3. अहंकार                      15. अव्यक्त

4. गुण                          16. धारण

5. ज्ञान                         17. आत्मन्

6. कुरुक्षेत्र                    18. आनन्द

7. कर्म                          19. अष्टाङ्गयोग

8. ध्यान                        20. तत्त्वमसि

9. दर्शन                         21. नामरूप

10. दुःख                        22. उपनिषद्

11. अभ्यङ्ग                     23. नित्य

12. चित्त                        24. धर्म

Answers:

| | |
|---|---|
| 1. ṛṣi | 13. citta-vṛtti |
| 2. āsana | 14. avidyā |
| 3. ahaṃkāra | 15. avyakta |
| 4. guṇa | 16. dhāraṇa |
| 5. jñāna | 17. ātman |
| 6. Kuru-kṣetra | 18. ānanda |
| 7. karma | 19. aṣṭāṅga-yoga |
| 8. dhyāna | 20. tat tvam asi |
| 9. darśana | 21. nāma-rūpa |
| 10. duḥkha | 22. Upaniṣad |
| 11. abhyaṅga | 23. nitya |
| 12. citta | 24. dharma |

Pronounce the following words:

1. पुराण

2. राम

3. पुरुष

4. प्रकृति

5. प्रज्ञा

6. सीता

7. सुखम्

8. संयम

9. संसार

10. संस्कार

11. संस्कृत

12. सत्यम्

13. रामराज्य

14. रामायण

15. शिष्य

16. स्थितप्रज्ञ

17. भगवद्गीता

18. समाधि

19. योग

20. बुद्ध

21. महाभारत

22. प्रज्ञापराध

23. वेदान्त

24. वेदलीला

Answers:

| | |
|---|---|
| 1.  Purāṇa | 13. rāma-rājya |
| 2.  Rāma | 14. Rāmāyaṇa |
| 3.  puruṣa | 15. śiṣya |
| 4.  prakṛti | 16. sthita-prajña |
| 5.  prajñā | 17. Bhagavad-Gītā |
| 6.  Sītā | 18. samādhi |
| 7.  sukham | 19. yoga |
| 8.  saṃyama | 20. Buddha |
| 9.  saṃsāra | 21. Mahābhārata |
| 10. saṃskāra | 22. prajñāparādha |
| 11. Saṃskṛta | 23. Vedānta |
| 12. satyam | 24. Veda-Līlā |

**READING FROM THE BHAGAVAD-GĪTĀ**

Now that you've learned the rules of pronunciation, practice pronouncing and reading the script with selections from the **Bhagavad-Gītā**. You could read in the roman script and then cover it and read the **devanāgarī** script:

निस्त्रैगुण्यो भवार्जुन

nistraiguṇyo bhavārjuna
Be without the three gunas, O Arjuna,

निर्द्वन्द्वो

nirdvandvo
freed from duality,

नित्यसत्त्वस्थो

nitya-sattvastho
ever firm in purity,

नियोगक्षेम

niryoga-kṣema
independent of possessions,

आत्मवान्

ātmavān
possessed of the Self.

*Bhagavad-Gītā*, 2.45

योगस्थः कुरु कर्माणि

yogasthaḥ kuru karmāṇi

Established in Yoga perform actions,


सङ्गं त्यक्त्वा धनञ्जय

saṅgaṃ tyaktvā dhanañjaya

having abandoned attachment, O winner of wealth,


सिद्ध्यसिद्ध्योः समो भूत्वा

siddhy-asiddyoḥ samo bhūtvā

having become balanced in success and failure,


समत्वं योग उच्यते

samatvaṃ yoga ucyate

for balance of mind is called Yoga.

*Bhagavad-Gītā*, 2.48

योगः कर्मसु कौशलम्

yogaḥ karmasu kauśalam

Yoga is skill in action.

*Bhagavad-Gītā*, 2.50

नियतं कुरु कर्म त्वम्

niyataṃ kuru karma tvam

Do your allotted duty.

*Bhagavad-Gītā*, 3.8

गाहना कर्मनो गतिः

gāhanā karmano gatiḥ

Unfathomable is the course of action.

*Bhagavad-Gītā*, 4.17

धर्मक्षेत्रे कुरुक्षेत्रे समवेता

dharma-kṣetre kuru-kṣetre samavetā

Assembled on the field of Dharma, on the field of the Kurus.

*Bhagavad-Gītā*, 1.1

न हि ज्ञानेन सदृशं पवित्रमिह विद्यते

na hi jñānena sadṛśaṁ pavitram iha vidyate
Truly there is in this world nothing so purifying as
knowledge.

*Bhagavad-Gītā*, 4.38

स निश्चयेन योक्तव्यो योगो

ऽनिर्विण्णचेतसा

sa niścayena yoktavyo yogo 'nirviṇṇa-cetasā
This Yoga should be practised with firm resolve and heart
undismayed.

*Bhagavad-Gītā*, 6.23

The apostrophe ( ' ), written in **devanāgarī** by **ऽ**, represents the
missing letter **a**. See **Introduction to Sanskrit**, p. 90, number 8.

प्रसादे सर्वदुःखानां हानिरस्योपजायते

prasāde sarva-duḥkhānāṁ hānirasyopajāyte
In "grace" is born an end to all his sorrows.

*Bhagavad-Gītā*, 2.65

क्षिप्रं हि मानुषे लोके सिद्धिर्भवति कर्मजा

kṣipraṃ hi mānuṣe loke siddhir bhavati karmajā
For success born of action comes quickly in the world of men.

*Bhagavad-Gītā*, 4.12

सर्वं कर्माखिलं पार्थ ज्ञाने परिसमाप्यते

sarvaṃ karmākhilaṃ pārtha jñāne parisamāpyate
All action without exception, O Partha, culminates in knowledge.

*Bhagavad-Gītā*, 4.33

स शान्तिमधिगच्छति

sa śāntim adhigacchati
He attains to peace.

*Bhagavad-Gītā*, 2.71

यं लब्ध्वा चापरं लाभं मन्यते नाधिकं ततः

yaṃ labdhvā cāparaṃ lābhaṃ manyate nādhikaṃ tataḥ
Having gained which he counts no other gain as higher.

*Bhagavad-Gītā*, 6.22

ज्ञानं लब्ध्वा परां शान्तिमचिरेणाधिगच्छति

jñānaṃ labdhvā parāṃ śāntim
acireṇādhigacchati

Having gained knowledge, swiftly he comes to the
supreme peace.

*Bhagavad-Gītā*, 4.39


योगयुक्तो मुनिर्ब्रह्म न चिरेणाधिगच्छति

yoga-yukto munir brahma na cireṇādhigacchati
The sage who is intent on Yoga comes to Brahman
without long delay.

*Bhagavad-Gītā*, 5.6


इहैव तैर्जितः सर्गो येषां साम्ये स्थितं मनः

ihaiva tair jitaḥ sargo yeṣāṃ sāmye sthitaṃ
manaḥ

Even here, in this life, the universe is conquered by those
whose mind is established in equanimity.

*Bhagavad-Gītā*, 5.19

यो ऽन्तः सुखो ऽन्तरारामस्तथान्तज्यॉतिरेव

yo 'ntaḥ sukho 'ntarārāmas tathāntarjyotir eva
Whose happiness is within, whose contentment is
within, whose light is all within.

*Bhagavad-Gītā*, 5.24

स्थित्वा ऽस्यामन्तकाले ऽपि

ब्रह्मनिर्वाणमृच्छति

sthitvā 'syām anta-kāle 'pi brahma-nirvāṇam
ṛcchati
Established in that, even at the last moment, he attains
eternal freedom in divine consciousness.

*Bhagavad-Gītā*, 2.72

प्रशान्तमनसं ह्येनं योगिनं सुखमुत्तमम्

praśānta-manasaṃ hy enaṃ yoginaṃ sukham
uttamam
For supreme happiness comes to the yogi whose mind is
deep in peace.

*Bhagavad-Gītā*, 6.27

| | | | | | | | | | |
|---|---|---|---|---|---|---|---|---|---|
| **SANSKRIT** | svara | अ a | आ ā | | | | | | |
| **ALPHABET** | | इ i | ई ī | | | | | | |
| | | उ u | ऊ ū | | | | | | |
| | | ऋ ṛ | ॠ ṝ | | | | | | |
| | | ऌ ḷ | | | | | | | |
| | | ए e | ऐ ai | | | | | | |
| | | ओ o | औ au | | | | | | |

| | | | | | |
|---|---|---|---|---|---|
| anusvāra | अं aṃ (ṃ) | visarga | | अः aḥ (ḥ) | |
| jihvāmūlīya | ⊁ ẖ | upadhmānīya | | ⊁ ḫ | |

| sparśa | क ka | ख kha | ग ga | घ gha | ङ ña |
|---|---|---|---|---|---|
| | च ca | छ cha | ज ja | झ jha | ञ ña |
| | ट ṭa | ठ ṭha | ड ḍa | ढ ḍha | ण ṇa |
| | | | ळ ḷa | ळ्ह ḷha | |
| | त ta | थ tha | द da | ध dha | न na |
| | प pa | फ pha | ब ba | भ bha | म ma |
| antaḥstha | | य ya | र ra | ल la | व va |
| ūṣman | | श śa | ष ṣa | स sa | ह ha |